Train to Agra

CRAB ORCHARD AWARD
SERIES IN POETRY

First Book Award

D0937798

TRAIN
TO
AGRA

Vandana Khanna

Crab Orchard Review
&
Southern Illinois University Press

CARBONDALE AND
EDWARDSVILLE

Printed in the United States of America

04   03   02   01   4   3   2   1

The Crab Orchard Award Series in Poetry is a joint publishing venture of Southern Illinois University Press and *Crab Orchard Review.* This series has been made possible by the generous support of the Office of the President of Southern Illinois University and the Office of the Vice Chancellor for Academic Affairs and Provost at Southern Illinois University Carbondale.

Crab Orchard Award Series in Poetry Editor: Jon Tribble

Text design by Erin Kirk New

Library of Congress Cataloging-in-Publication Data

Khanna, Vandana, 1972–
Train to Agra / Vandana Khanna.
p. cm. — (Crab Orchard award series in poetry)
1. India—Poetry. 2. East Indian Americans—Poetry. I. Title. II. Series.
PS3611.H36 T7 2001
811'.54—dc21
ISBN 0-8093-2405-9 (alk. paper)   2001018375

The paper used in this publication meets the minimum requirements of American National Standard for Information Sciences—Permanence of Paper for Printed Library Materials, ANSI Z39.48-1992. ∞

For My Family

Contents

Acknowledgments

Grateful acknowledgment is made to the editors of the following publications in which poems in this book originally appeared, sometimes in slightly different form:

Callaloo—"Hair," "Dot Head," and "Spell"
Crab Orchard Review—"The India of Postcards" and "Plums"
Crazyhorse—"Evening Prayer"
The Cream City Review—"Bowl"
First of the Month—"Lost"
Hanging Loose—"Alignment" and "Stardust"
Hawai'i Review—"Screens"
Hayden's Ferry Review—"Elephant God"
International Poetry Review—"Eyes"
International Quarterly—"Twentieth-Century Sita"
LIT—"Blackwater Fever" and "When My Father Didn't Work"
Puerto del Sol—"Bread"
Rattle—"Echo"
Sycamore Review—"4th Street Cemetery" and "Denali"
Third Coast Magazine—"Hence, Monsoon" and "On the Edge of Delhi"

I would like to extend my gratitude to my mentors and to all those who continue to inspire me: Rita Dove, Alyce Miller, David Wojahn, Maura Stanton, Cathy Bowman, and Charles Wright.

A special thanks to Allison Joseph for selecting this manuscript and to those in the M.F.A. program at Indiana University for their constant support and insight, especially: Tenaya Darlington, David Daniels, Karri Offstein, Susan Brown, and Angela Pneuman.

Finally, many thanks and much love to Jason, Sneh, and Vinod and to my entire family, both in India and America, without whom I would not be able to write.

Train to Agra

Train to Agra

I want to reach you—
in that city where the snow

only shimmers silver
for a few hours. It has taken

seventeen years. This trip,
these characters patterned

in black ink, curves catching
on the page like hinges,

this weave of letters fraying
like the lines on my palm,

all broken paths. Outside,
no snow. Just the slow pull

of brown on the hills, umber
dulling to a bruise until the city

is just a memory of stained teeth,
the burn of white marble

to dusk, cows standing
on the edges like a dust

cloud gaining weight
after days of no rain. Asleep

in the hot berth, my parents
sway in a dance, the silence

broken by scrape of tin, hiss
of tea, and underneath,

the constant clatter of wheels
beating steel tracks over and over:

to the city of white marble,
to the city of goats, tobacco

fields, city of dead hands,
a mantra of my grandmother's—

her teeth eaten away
by betel leaves—the story

of how Shah Jahan had cut off
all the workers' hands

after they built the Taj, so they
could never build again. I dreamt

of those hands for weeks before
the trip, weeks even before I

stepped off the plane, thousands
of useless dead flowers drying

to sienna, silent in their fall.
Every night, days before, I dreamt

those hands climbing over the iron
gate of my grandparents' house, over

grate and spikes, some caught
in the groove between its sharpened

teeth, others biting where
they pinched my skin.

ONE

Spell

for Lori

I thought it was the city, the muddled city.
Outside the car window—everything surging—

children scratching glass, never having seen anyone so pale,
broken animals, roads bitten away. India. When I look back

I will remember you crying in the heat of the car,
before we ever reached the Taj, before we climbed up

the steps, hot grass then cool marble under our feet. We thought
we had seen everything—the President's house, India Gate with its guards

and faded postcards, Quitar Minar, where the man pulled
your arms behind your back, around the pillar for good luck.

You hoped it was worth the ache in your back that followed.
We traveled the city like we didn't belong, a place I should call home

but as foreign to me as to you. And you? Who can say why you cried,
two miles from the Taj in the city proper. My aunt thought it was the heat.

Maybe it was roaming the cluttered streets, no face your own,
or that smell when we stepped off the plane—

mixture of petroleum, spice and dust. Or was it dusk?
Then there were the stares, the calls to come look,

glass bangles shaken at us like charms, like some spell,
and it was, with garlands stringing the runway like tiny beads of blood.

Blackwater Fever

They didn't find it in me until months later—
just like Vallejo who died on a rainy
day far from the heat rising over a garden
in silvers and reds—far away from the din
of buses, tobacco vendors, cows that overran
the streets with their holiness. Laid on the surface
of the Ganges, the thin shells reflected light, clamored
against the current. Far from the Atlantic, farther still
from the Potomac. Same color of night, dull dawn.
The fever should have churned my blood into tight
fists while the sunset stretched across the sky
like an open mouth. Everything was splintered heat.
I'd awake to winter in D.C., find streets covered
in snow, the words of some ancient language blooming
under my ankles like a song, a mantra called home.
I could trace it like a geography of someone I had once been.
How to explain the hum of mosquitos in my ear, sensual
and low, nothing like the sound of rusted-out engines,
police sirens, a train's whistle. How easily I'd lost the taste
for that water, opened my legs to their hot, biting mouths.

Thread

While men sit sipping
goat's milk under
the arms of the cucumber

tree, I lie on a cot
in the library, sweating
out the fever—cross-breeze

and fan, Austen and Shakespeare.
I gather dust like the government
files graying overhead, my hands

slowly eaten by the hot skillet, drying
like two pods, edges burned tight
and crisp, my breath dank after eating

betel leaves for days, teeth
stained to dull blood, and I think
of the city exhaling—carts, cars,

even the silk of saris before
wilting in the sun, static and sizzling,
the corn in corner markets

over coals, salted lemons rubbed
raw, blistering my lips, those days
waking to my hands wrapped

like two loaves, wrapped to keep
me from biting them, from breaking
skin. Days before the biting, before

the burns—waking to half-darkness,
candle wet with wax, then also
the smell of spoiled books, my fingers

wet across words, catching them
like rain, everything bending into corners,
my fingers over curve and bend of letters—

unfamiliar, alien, the words stale
in my mouth—hardened brittle bread.
The only words I remember are ones

of absence, letters like fish hooks,
crooked fingers scratching slick glass.
Outside the rumble of thunder clouds

like the rattle of tin cans rolling,
thousands of tin cans.

2.

The bandages peel like layers
of an onion, yellow from cloth

and heat. My cry is hollow,
the stone center of a mango

rattling, beading through
my throat. Each unraveling

is a thread, my hands buried
under the musk of burned leaves,

salve of wet soil, each finger an aching
branch blooming tips to night sky.

In the evenings, my aunt with balms
and clucking tongue holds the shadow

of skin, the patches of magenta,
passages of faded blue. She can trace

each ridge and burn like a path
with a slip of each slick finger.

I hear the low trills of men,
steely and thin through the glass

and click of overhead fan, men who
weave the night into nets, bowls

cupping sound from alleyways between
the house and squatter village, sagging

tarp, old wood fires dulled by rain.
I imagine their hands holding back

the swell of night—the current and undertow
of sounds like water, while mine lay drowning

under cloth and balms, ruined hands burned
by teeth marks, my voice unraveling,

shedding skin like the throat of a burned-out
magnolia simmering on the city's edge.

Eyes

Shedding—that's what they called it.
Those months of power shortages
when I was nine and woke to
splintered electricity, forced blindness,
the dark tasting of rust and stone
pressing itself against the house. My fingers

scraped screens, wooden doorways,
palms ribbed with their design and permanence
looking for bends in the smooth
line of wall, for stars on the steel plate
of night, the silver against black.

When I was born, my eyes swelled
from the hard birth, shunned light—
there was fear of scarring, fear of blindness.
My mother kept watch for a week,
willing the tight lids open. As a child,

I saw my great-aunt's cataract eyes
grayed by age as beautiful—not seeing
them for what they were: eyes drowning themselves,
weakening muscles crystallized, dulled
by misplaced clouds. It was the silence: no fan,

no fluorescent hum from the hallway, the absence
of sound and shadow that woke me, alone—
the only sleepwalker, nightwalker, ghost
in the house. We send money every fall

to Calcutta, buying eyes for those who
cannot see—the dark bruise of sight
settling the shadows. Somewhere an iris,
a pupil, a lens placed in my name.

Dun

The first time, when I was eight and could remember
the flight, I cried in the bathroom when I saw India
from thirty thousand feet, cried in the tight pocket between sink
and door after my brother pointed to the flat tracks
of brown, crusted edges like burnt bread, steel-lined
tracks gingered with age.

I had seen pictures, imagined the green teardrop of a map
lined with blue veins. Instead, everything looked flattened,
rubbed down by a rolling pin. I thought, I can't go; each rut
and curve would singe my feet. Everything lacked green,
not at all like the glossy world my mother had shown us
in the atlas, trying to orient, to give a picture.

Even now, with each dip and bend of the plane, my eyes long
for color, for shape, for something to identify and assign a name
to. Control tower, thatched roof, slim line of the Ganges.
Anything to place order on these small vines taking root
in muddied rivers, hard buds of color and water opening
to a garden of rusted flowers, burnished leaves.

Stardust

Under the heavy rope of my hair
I will wear a black dot on my nape

behind my left ear, but it won't save me.
It's supposed to ward off the evil eye,

stop anyone from stealing my happiness
with one glance. Even my aunt with a *Shree*

and an *Om* laying hands on me like a seer,
until I am a sacrament, something almost holy,

can't save me. The Ganesh on my desk, sent
from a crowded street stall, sent by a woman

who knows about luck, who can see good
fortune in a damp palm, in the set of someone's

teeth, won't do any good. I've prayed to Ganesh,
Mr. Good Luck himself, spent time laying flowers

and rice at his steely feet, yet nothing can change
how the set of the stars writes my story.

My mother prays every night to the monkey god,
the god of her household, as I try to reconstruct

the past—reading more from the shape of a seven,
the curve of a two than anyone intended—and it's hard.

Reconstructing. Inventing. Putting things back into place,
out of place, out of time. I'm making things up. Anything

to cheat the stars, that old astrologer's poor sight.
I can hear my aunt praying into my hair, oiling

it to a fine rain in her hands. Each tug tells me
not to forget the dust beneath my feet, the fan clicking

its head like a negligent bird turning
to catch sight, ruffling us with its breath.

On the Edge of Delhi

I am the one who is afraid of the dark,
afraid of the cornfields on the edge
of my aunt's farm, the ones that whisper
at night long after the last train whistle
shakes the house and after my uncle
falls asleep from too much whiskey
and not enough meat. Your voice is thick
with iambs, husks opened to the night, mouths
hiding rows of hard, beaded secrets. You tell
me about Krishna and the cows, about Pravathi
carving her son from mud. Every night
it is a different story: Ganesh running
through the jungle, Sita swallowed by the ground.
It always comes back to the one who rides
the tiger, the one who is unafraid of fire.
You speak in a language that seems to love
the tongue. You would do anything
to keep me from thinking I am in exile,
to keep me from the shadows that bend
and curve, that make the night
seem closer than it is.

The India of Postcards

We began in one corner of the city
and plowed through cows and dung
and scooters, marbled and dusted
streets to the other. We were high
on heat and medicine. Anything
to protect our ourselves from disease,
and there were so many—cholera, malaria,
meningitis. All sounding soft and beautiful
on our lips, full of vowels and danger.
The only thing we wanted we couldn't have:
water—unbottled, unboiled—pure, sweet,
American-tasting water. With every sip,
a prayer to one of the gods: the god of good
health and an easy flight home, the god of
treasures hidden away in crowded street stalls.
There were other things, of course—trinkets
made of colored glass, hand-painted boxes, raw
silk—anything to say we had been there. Something
to hang on the walls of our tiny apartments. We were
looking for the gods, for the one thing
that shimmered more than silver, a pyramid
or temple, a country—something we couldn't fit
into our pockets. We wanted the India of postcards
with our faces on the front. Under all that glitter,
we wanted the shards of something we can't name.

TWO

Against Vallejo

I will die in Ireland on a cold day on the coast
when the sea burns against darkening rock
and the mist hangs low over hills. It will be
a Sunday because Sundays are days of rest
and worship and because I have worked
a lifetime only to have my spine ready to snap.

I have never seen Ireland, and my family
will not understand my longing for swift wind
smarting my skin, my fingernails turning
the blue of cornflowers. I will want to be burned
like a true Hindu, my soul set free of this jaded
body, this broken vase—so my skin can mist
and my bones crack, splinter like burning wood.

Vandana Khanna is dead. They will not understand
me far away from the heat and dust of Delhi, cloistered
in a damp room, my fingers stiff from writing.
This after years of thirst, years shivering under woolen
shawls brought back from Kashmir. They will not
understand you, feverish, whispering Spanish words
into my mouth because I love the way
vowels sound against your lips.

Or rather, I will die in Spain on a Sunday afternoon
when the stores have closed for the sun, men sitting
in the shade of a magnolia outside my window,
sipping from cold oranges, cut and soaked in sugar
water. I have never been to Spain but will want
that heat, reminding me of my home. I will die
from the inside out, a fever turning my veins gray,
thighs bruising easily like fruit.

And you will spread my body out like a cool sheet,
cover my hands with henna, thread my body with beads,
and no one will understand why but you, because I
have worked a lifetime, and today I am tired of metaphors,
of empty leaves that rain like ash.

Two Women

We squat in the cool grass gnawing
sugar cane. Brackish water brushes

the soles of our feet—your hair smells
of cloves—skin the color of sandalwood.

We talk of our men lost
in wars, lost in other women,

and of the children we gained:
sons, grandsons, daughters.

The sahib's wife calls, the green shutters
are open, and Verdi drifts

in the air around us.
It is time to shake out

the dust-clogged rug,
clean the brandy glasses,

and feed the remains
to the waiting dogs.

The Nook

Each dusk, I return to the curve
of the cucumber tree where my grandparents

first drank tea under the eyes
of their matchmaker, matching lip prints

on the same cup: the first and last
time they met before the wedding,

before seven times around the burning wood,
before rain-drums and the wedding dye painting

their hands. I curl with grass-licked legs
under the weave of branches, my knees

in wet mud. My spine cracks as I lean
to bend my lips to the trunk, feeling

the sharpness of bark, nothing like the taste
of silver smooth against my tongue.

Against Tu Fu

Twenty years to reach
this house, this night of leeks
smarting in our hands.
Silver combs our hair
after these many years
of the scratch of wool skirts,
starched shirts. We

bend over wild shoots
in your garden, muddied
ankles in this even muddier
night, rain beading moisture
into the air, into skin. We

cut spring onions for soup.
They are young with rain, speak
between dulled knife edges
of friends like sun-dried stalks,
how they've lost the sharpness

of shallots. Your children ask
my name, where I come from.
Inside, limp strands pepper
in the light, candle and lamp ease
the corners of our faces. We

eat, our feet warmed by wood
and wine. Your children leave
us, glasses in hand, each one
a cup of blue roses. We drink deeply
from its throat. So many names—
radish, millet, leek—trying to curve
the soil back from places I've stepped,
rain smearing the imprint.

Hence, Monsoon

They watch each evening for rain,
the dry lightning—momentary blindness.
The boy arrives again to sweep the floors,
beat screens free of dust and flies. Twice
each day, he cleans, and still the house creaks,
mellows under the skin of the city, a shadow
that rusts each corner and basin.

On bamboo chairs with cushions that ease
the pain of brittle bones, they sit and shell
peanuts among the rosebugs.

Through open windows, lizards flee
the sun, cling to cool walls
as everything waits for the sound
of water slipping off the leaves,
the monsoon rain singing on marble floors.

Domes

We should have gone on the train, the way
for travelers, tourists, ones who don't belong.

I wanted a map of Agra, you wanted India
for your postcards—all the colors, stories

to tell your friends back in Boston.
We were hungry for all of it: the city

pressing against the car doors, the story
of the Taj that found its way into our dreams.

Whatever happened to all those hands taken
from the workers, from those who built the Taj,

step by step, sealing slabs of marble together
with their sweat? We were blinded when the sun

first shone on it just like in the postcards, blinded
like the architect who designed it, so he could

only see it once, ordered to never build again,
only his mind remembering the color of marble

like teeth. My aunt tells us this story over a lunch
of spiced cabbage and bread at a roadside stand

on the way, of the emperor years later imprisoned
by his son, desperately pulling his hair out by strands,

clogging his water basin. Every night until his death,
he watched the moon set over the domes

from his prison cell, watched by mirror as
the reflection reversed, closed in on itself.

Alignment

In Hindi, love is always the long version:
"You are in my heart." In Hindi movies,
you can tell always it's a love scene because the man
and woman never kiss, just sing and gyrate
their hips towards each other. Love is splashed
like billboards all along the Delhi streets in a blur
of reds and blues.

Every time my grandmother tried to learn how
to drive, she got pregnant. She never learned
how to shift gears, but she had three children.

I know the lines give me away. My palms hold
all the stories: you will lose like your mother
and great-grandmother, like all the women
in your family, all of them widows.

My grandmother at thirteen: married a man
she had never seen before the wedding day,
before the fire and the pundit. Fifty years
later, my grandmother at sixty-three:
"That was not the best way but the only way."

Before the wedding, before years of marriage,
my parents consulted an astrologer to see
if their stars were aligned. Thirty years
of marriage based on stardust and heat.
Love is all numbers. The math insists upon it.

The Palm Reader

Your neck stretches like the stalks of young corn,
like the stems of sunflowers, and your eyes are fresh
like berries. You will live in a quiet village, near

a lake and mountains, where people sit at dusk,
feel the cool breeze on their necks before sleep,
where they watch for lightning, a sign of a coming storm.

I never saw the lake, my view of the night sky eclipsed
by brick tenements, the mountains of skyscrapers
drowning me in their shadow. I lived most of my life

in a one room apartment, in a building where English
was everyone's second language, where the train
rattled windows every morning at four.

You were born in the month of the monsoons,
where the snow melts on the Himalayas and spreads
its fingers, where the cow's moan drowns out
the cicada.

I never went back, after a childhood of chills and fevers,
the country rejecting my body. There is so much between
us now: buildings and streets, cows, tigers, water and people
and people. *Your palms hold the broken paths of your life*

together. She said, *your skin is whitening, your eyes*
are losing their shape, you must return or you will suffer,
and I have because I can't remember the words
for love, apple, want.

Twentieth-Century Sita

1.

I never learned about sex from my mother,
a woman who didn't know what the word
whore meant in English, or from Hindi movies
with all their thrust and grind but no kisses,
no nudity—the camera hovering over parted
lips that never seemed to touch. I never learned
the first time with Charles in the back room
of my house. We were just tongue-heavy mouths
and that was it. No fevered breath in my ear,
no one breaking into song.

2.

The second time was after midnight
under an apple tree. He said, *the first time
I saw you, I thought you were white,* and leaned
in. He was the last Indian I ever kissed,
but once, another read me the *Kama Sutra*
by lamplight, pointed out the diagrams.

3.

My mother speaks of broken teacups, half moons
of regret, and I am never sure if she means sex
or spilling tea. She spends Saturdays fingering
classifieds in the back of *India Today* for a suitable
suitor. Their stats say it all in fifteen words or less
(read as Indian, Hindu, Punjabi).

Now, I've thrown off the *purdah* for good,
and it's nothing but banishment for me. She hopes
some Ram will ask me to walk through the wedding fire
like a modern day Sita in blue jeans to prove my purity,
to prove I didn't want anything but a monkey god to save me.

Aurora

It called us out of the shadow of the mountains—
from the house, the gravel road winding
through town, into the fields thick with moose

and fireweed. We looked for it in the museum
at Fairbanks, in between totems and bear skin,
the light caught on the blues of the television screen.

It was there and not there—lingering over us, a halo
hovering above the surface of the earth. I imagine
it covering us with its frayed fingers in the dark,

as we squat in the wet grass bordering the Chena,
the truck's headlights making our breath
glisten. We searched for it in the wrong season,

like Halley who thought he would die
before he saw it, or perhaps die seeing it.
It was the wrong season, and that is the point.

Bathed in summer's last sun, hands wrapped
against the cool dampness, our faces wrapped
against mosquitos, we wanted to be shocked

by electricity, by flame—flushed red with wanting,
our feet soaked in river water and mud, wanted
to watch it grow bright over ice as foretold

by clairvoyants, astronomers, Indians. But no ice,
nothing shattered the sky. We heard stories of its
attraction knocking out power lines that picketed

the sky, eating lights away from homes
where the field was the strongest. Heard of how
it got into dogs' hair, making their coats snap

and spark, stand on end. We had traveled far—
rolled the name on our tongues like sweetness,
like Galileo once did in a dream, uncurling

from his mouth into the world. We had driven
miles into the bush, backs against bluebells
and wild roses, our breath magnetic

in the light, tangible between wet grass
 and darkness. We waited for color to thread
the sky, to spit with sound even though science

can't prove the crackling, the hiss that Eskimos
have heard for centuries—denying light and sound
could occur at the selfsame time. We waited for it

to glisten and flicker, tried to beckon it with our whistle,
with the quiet rubbing of our hands.

Denali

On the bus, I was always looking the wrong way.
Waking on and off to *mertensia* and *potentila,* we called

them foxtail and wild roses, finding a name for that color
against the slate of rock. We were heading towards the tundra—

wind rattled our teeth—heading to the park where whole states
could lose themselves. Outside, the Nenana tumbled past,

making us see nothing but what was in front of us, not the possibilities
of muddy water, of rocks the color of river, not the shape of rapids

and how easily they could snag a line, pull us under. We awoke
to sheep on the mountainside, a grizzly and her cubs, all caught

in the blurred space of window, clotted with thumbprints
of tourists who had come before us, all trying to catch nature,

so our eyes would remember, so we could tell stories.
The moose and caribou, how they were all browns and dark flesh,

tight muscles drawn to bone. Waiting for nature to hit us
with its shape and permanence, I could never find the speck

on the side of the mountain, the one that said, *I am bear, I am cub.*
Bad at focusing, my eyes tricked me—what I thought were goats, Dahl

sheep, were really just two curves of rock. I was always looking
away, catching movement where there was none.

4th Street Cemetery

It was those walks through the graveyard that mattered,
that and the donuts fresh baked at midnight. We could
smell the sugar in the air all the way from the edge
of the cemetery grounds, how everything was heavy with it—
the leaves, the grass, even the limestone seemed to glisten
with its shadings under the moon, making you want to touch
them, stick your fingers in your mouth. The smell
was so strong, our tongues swelled with longing, our stomachs
throbbed and made us crazy, and we crept under weeping willows
and cypress, passed headstones named Nutty and Brown just
for the sugar, the chocolate and glazed. We swore we could
hear whispers, dogs barking as if from behind us, muffled by
death, dirt, and leaves. And sometimes mud stuck to our shoes,
sucking the ground every time we lifted our feet, the sound almost
of gasping breath, sure to wake those lying around us. We made sure
to walk on edges, staying away from the thick mounds freshly dug.
We wanted only to make it through the grass and death and night
to the neon sign, to the sweetness.

THREE

Screens

We are ten, girls whose families
left Delhi behind in winter, Assam

in the summer. The ones who spent Saturday
mornings feeling our feet slap cold tile floors,

stirring up the dust above the Korean grocery
where our mothers haggled over almonds

and rice. We are taught the steps
by a woman with a thick Bengali accent

that makes us laugh. We mimic her lilt,
her steps. And for hours, our feet sing

with hers, each shiver of ankle warming
the floor as we go. We pretend not to understand,

make her repeat herself. We are difficult, want
nothing of what our families left behind, long for

names that are easy on the tongue, afternoons
at the mall, dances with boys in the dark corners

of school gymnasiums. We had grown up seeing
our mothers, their bellies firm and bare in photos,

as still lifes in black-and-white—henna rusting
on their hands, on thumbs and palms,

no color back then, just their words filling them in.
We had grown up with heavy silk saris waiting for us

in our mother's closets, waiting to bend
our backs, to trace the curve of India

on our spines. In the back rooms of our houses,
their steps muffled in blue-gray carpeting,

the low swing of hips outlined by the heat
of the TV screen, our mothers mirrored

the motions of silver-clad women, mouthed
lyrics, rings slicing the air—translating

each step from the nineteen-inch into 3-D,
their arms in some ancient dialect

that we hadn't learned the words to.
Palms cupped outward, fingers curled—

this means *wait,* this one *come closer.*
But words lose themselves on my limbs,

confused somewhere between forearm
and wrist, wrist and fingers. I was trying

to learn. I would say *come closer*
when I meant *wait, look at me.*

Blue Madonna

Back before color threaded
the world, when everything
was in black-and-white, I was
the only pagan at school, hiding
my breath with its curry and accent,
mouthing words to prayers I didn't
understand. I wondered why there
were always holy men but so few holy
women. I wanted to be enchanted,
to steal the baby Jesus from the Christmas
play and keep him hidden in my closet,
pull him out when I needed to be saved.
I wanted to be the blue Madonna holding
all the pieces of her son together.

Half a world away, girls my age came
as close to God as anyone could be.
They were already throwing their bodies
over their husband's funeral pyres, flung
out like blankets over the flames, chanting
Ram, Ram like a nursery rhyme. My mother
told me it was a holy mantra, the more I said
it, the holier I would be, but I never really knew
how or why, just that it was supposed to happen.
Once I tried saying it as many times as I could
in fifty seconds, but nothing. No miracle,
no halo of thorns around my head. And all I
could think about were those girls, widows
at fifteen. What did burning flowers smell like?
Something terrible, something holy?

Lost

Our house in America overlooked the neat grids
of the parking lot, the tired sycamores, ring-stained
pool. A one room apartment with a fold-out couch
for my brother and me. The hallways were always dark
with the smell of beer, chili powder, and fried bananas.
Voices scraped down the walls from each closed door,
reminding us of somewhere we had once been.
That's where we found replacements for everything,
where my mother lost her accent, spent hours every night
pressing saris into place, straightening their indigo
and marigold. She spent years in night school
beating out her life with each stroke of the typewriter,
the quick click of the egg timer reminding us of months
we had spent eating boiled eggs and soup, no money
for frying pans, for rolling pins. She always said we had
a big house in Green Park—lemon trees out front, a stone
wall blocking out the sounds of motor-scooters, cabbage
vendors, camels. I ruined my mother's one chance
of going back home. I was a dowry ready to be spent.
Here, the train's tumble through town rattles the windows.
She says it sounds like sugar cane rustling, except louder.

Plums

All summer I'd wait for the brown to spread
over my skin like dusk. We were fifteen,
sucking on plum pits till they were stones rattling
our mouths. There was the Christmas pageant
where we danced down the aisle to the Hail Mary,
and there was the avenue where boys would ride
in the back of pickups, and that was all there was.
They'd call out to us in Spanish, something
that must have meant kiss or hips, something
that was soft on the lips and behind the ears.
We didn't understand the words or the thrust
behind them, just thought of dark corners
of a room. Something smoky and smooth
on the radio. Filling our lungs with honeysuckle,
with the smell of summer, smell of something
we thought was sex. At home my mother wrapped
her body in silk scarves that were heavy with the musk
of a far off land I had only heard stories of, a skin
she was trying to push herself back into
with all its dust and diesel, sugar cane and spice.

Elephant God

If I were a good Hindu, I would believe
as my mother does—that ashes sprinkled
in the Potomac River will somehow reach

the Ganges—that my father, reborn,
is somewhere in the world, someone else's
husband, father. Or maybe I have it all wrong

and he is a daughter, not Indian or Hindu,
just living in a cold city near a river that flows back
upon itself. I am waiting for a sign, like you

calling from Delhi to say the wooden elephants
are drinking goat's milk. All over the country, people
spoon it into tusks and mouth. The milk's slow trickle

cracking thick skin, the wood brittle as teeth, blessed,
ready to snap. And it's something like religion—behind
carved wood, ivory tusks, there is something

drinking, someone listening to prayers with milk. I wait
for the day a postcard left in my mailbox will say
"Yes I am here, it is wonderful." Every hang up

on my answering machine is him calling
over and over just for the need to say
he is somewhere in the world. I will ask,

"Is the river really that color of night?" and whisper
words in my childhood tongue, something like *Ram, Ram,*
something like *make me holy.*

The Taming

The Sisters of the Sacred Heart
spent hours on my scrawl—cracking
knuckles into shape, pinching the back
of my hand—while outside the world of
St. James School, in the melting asphalt,
the air tight with cicadas, my father's heart
skipped a beat. How strange the pencil
felt after a long summer of boys freckling
in the sun, color threading my skin through
and through. In the hot rooms of September,
the sisters willed my Ss and Ls, tamed my unruly
fingers over thick paper curled brown
at the edges. Hands rode over mine, practicing
perfection. At night, I duplicated
shape and form while the monitor traced
my father's heart in ridges and valleys I couldn't
understand, could not translate. I wanted to order
each word into salvation, to write out the jagged,
scratch it into clean lines and half spaces.

Bowl

My head in the basket of her folded thighs,
she rubbed my hair, fingers thick from kneading
wheat bread that sold quickly at Sunday markets.
Flat cushions firm on my scalp, wrists that smelled
of vanilla and coconut oil.

She left my father in the hospital, left his breath
falling through the air, and slipped under the hot
sheets of my bed. It was then she let her bones
sigh against the painted wall of my room, her spine
like the trunk of a mango tree, curving.

Sometimes she spoke of things that could not be touched,
told stories I could eat, burning my throat
as the words went down.

Mostly, she cupped my head like a bowl asking
to be filled, listened to car horns and cicadas
through my window, undid the braid in her hair.
It fell around us sharply—
silver-black as rain under streetlights.

Bread

At home, no one saw me—my mother stirring
a pot of curry and rice, my father in shawls
reciting words in front of the TV set. I was nine.
I wanted to be a nun, to taste the dullness of bread
melting in my mouth. I wanted to feel stiff cotton
straighten my back, holy water on my lips,
fingers that ached for smooth glass beads sliding,
not the strangeness of sandalwood, not the almonds
of parents and grandparents, only the coolness
of dark pews, the gardenia's smell
and the silver crucifix against my wrists.

No one saw the soft edges curl
into the shape of my fingers, bread
sliced and curled into the womb of my palm.

I would unfold a blue napkin, its crisp leaves
stiff over my head, and tear into the bread,
leaving the remains an open mouth with nothing to say,
my lips in a secret mantra
I had watched the priests chant every Friday.

The soft coin rested on my tongue
as I'd heard Sister Miriam tell us:
Just let it rest there until it dissolves
like dew on morning grass
right when the sun hits it.
I sat there feeling my mouth
grow hot, listening to my mother
stir the rice and eggplant in the kitchen,
the scrape of steel spoon against iron
slice into my father's voice.

A Miracle in Blue Jeans

Somewhere far from me in towns called Normal
and Bethlehem, a girl in a coma is granting people
miracles. All day long visitors throng her bedroom
like rosary beads on wrists, lining it with their bodies,
wheelchairs, and holy water. Her hair has grown over
the edge of the bed, sweeping the floor. Some have cut
a piece and tucked it in their pockets. They have come
so the girl's mother can lift her hand and lay it
somewhere—head for tumors, wrists for arthritis,
spine for something growing like a bird's nest that
weaves itself larger every day. They have waited for a year
with their wounds of faith, kneeling in the driveway,
the gravel biting into soft knees. They wait for something
to cry the smell of roses, for a miracle in blue jeans,
for the day when the girl is laid out like the last supper
on a football field.

2.

Today, the computer programmer from Seattle
will play the part of Jesus. It took him two months
to grow out his beard, hair cascading just past his shoulders
as he becomes the image he has memorized from his second
grade religion textbook—the one where the plague of locusts
covers the sky like a dark cloak. The cross must be weighed
exactly, the dimensions in their recognized perfection.
How heavy? he thinks. It does not matter, not really,
as he must carry it—five pounds, twenty pounds, fifty pounds.
He must bear it. He was chosen. The air is dry with heat and death.

His wife will play Mary Magdalene, and she is disappointed
not to be the blue virgin. But at least she gets to wipe
his face, memorize eyes and nose with sweat and cloth. She will
stand out in the crowd. All the night before, she has prepared,
the moment when he will stop and she will step out, cloth extended.
Everything matters. She wishes she could wash his feet, but that
is another story, one before hers. He wishes it into being—the first
stumble, the smell of eucalyptus in the air. Everyone has memorized
their role—this one must call out, that one spit at his feet.

You Who Have Taken the Name Clare

At night, I can see the lights of the cloister
dimmed by trees, smell the dust and holy water
burning your wrists. Your gray cloak of silence

eclipsed by ten feet of stone and mortar, the wall
of holiness, wall of God—I think of that year you left us,
our English class mute with your decision, your longing

for silence, for rough work. For days after, your voice dissolved
under your tongue, brown bread sticking to your teeth.
How your fingertips dulled to a shine by hours of spinning thread,

hours of sowing open mouths closed. You left us to Austen
and Shakespeare, to reciting sonnets out loud, while you learned
to love the absence of sound, absence of an aching voice rubbed

raw, your world just a whisper, a holy name uttered
before sleep and dreams of burning, dreams of St. Clare,
your namesake, on the mountainside, of her sipping

from St. Francis's nipple, dropping her bowl of hot water, of food.
In the mornings, your skin is wet with unspoken things. You are
her daughter. You are chosen, hair falling under shears like words

stolen from your mouth. They are stolen, delicious, pushing through
the grated windows, between bits of stone and glass, mica glistening
under the moon. For days after you left, I chanted, loving the sound

of my voice, seduced with its timbre and substance—*cloister, cloister*—
until my tongue memorized the shape, soft mud and hard stone, a word
leaning into itself. As if by saying it, made it real—the stone wall,

the towers and oaken pews of your life. And what of us left behind,
wondering if your lips forgot their movement, if your tongue lost
its shape. Wondering if you whisper your name to make it your own.

Hunger

As a child, I wanted to be a martyr—breasts
on a platter, eyes gouged by ravens. I refused
to eat, and I thought that made me holy. At school,
the Sisters of the Immaculate Heart starved
themselves—thin and brittle as dried sugar cane—
and they were holy. I hungered to belong, wanted
my body eaten away, line and bone erased.
Afternoons in the cloister, I would watch them,
hidden behind mop or broom, scrubbing my way
towards heaven. They were all sharp angles, ghosts.
I was an echo, a girl whose parents believed in monkey
gods. Chanting names of saints, names of fruit, my mouth
was tight with the longing to taste some vow, something
sweet like holy water, like nothing.

When My Father Didn't Work

He'd squat under the magnolia just beginning
    to blossom and recite mantras, refusing to speak to me
        in English—those days, between jobs, the heat settling in for the afternoon,

cracked shells in his palm, his time scattered like peanuts in grass.
    His memories were both the mango's soft flesh
        and splintered glass bangles: a childhood in Lahore

before the city broke itself in two with its burned-out roofs
    and shards of glass, the smell of kerosene and fear,
        before dreams of men with dark knives who cut

the country in jagged lines—when the evenings were of cold water
    baths, Hindi movies, and sweet tea. His words turn back
        over themselves—time compacts them as though on a page,

or in the rough fibers of cloth—I see his rush from Lahore: the tight hours
    of packing in early morning, down the clattered streets
        from his house above the tailor's shop, the city closing in

upon itself, smoke trailing after him, erasing names from a map.
    He teaches me the smell of that earth, that country's
        particular odor of black tea and chilies, cow dung and tumeric.

He warns me of the arcade's dark mystery of music and men,
    telling me how some stories
        are broken shells, others knots in cloth.

Hair

Always the sound of knots tearing,
the scratch of hair against metal.
Those summer evenings when I'd go by

Anu's apartment on the floor above mine,
#406, and watch her mother tug at her hair
with a steel-toothed comb, their room

smelled of coconut oil and meat
left over from dinner. She can't cut it—ever.
And so, every night is a tug of war

with her mother, whose brown fingers
pull and rub, spreading it out like a sheet
against her back. Anu's father would laugh

at my skin, telling me to drink black tea,
sit in the sun, darken up, and let my hair grow
beyond my nape at least, his fingers

at the edge of my shirt collar. He'd never felt
the edges of a scissors' blade—his full gray beard
and hair mixing in a weave of silver-black—

a patchwork, a lifetime of wants, which he rolled
around the perimeter of his head and chin,
ending in a tight fist at the top. Her mother

whispered words into Anu's scalp and neck,
with each strand, a different story—of *American boys*
and *dances*, where skin touched, hair swayed

down backs, of the mythic Sita walking into fire
to prove her purity. We knew about *American boys*—
how there were none in our neighborhood,

how they'd ride by on bikes, and we'd watch them
from our bedroom windows and sometimes
from the front steps—their clean-skinned cheekbones,

smooth chests. All the while, Anu would move between
her mother's thighs like the fireflies we'd catch
in pickle jars, clicking and igniting in glass.

Dot Head

They caught us once between
the cypress trees, a block
from our apartment complex where

the hallways always smelled of beer
and boiled rice; though I don't remember
exactly, just two boys on bikes, the flash

of sunlight on steel handlebars, words
sharp, and the bite of mosquitos
that burned our ankles. Something hard

hit my brother in the head. A red *bindi*
in the center of his forehead like a rose,
like the ones I saw my mother wear, but

his bled down his face. A dot head,
a sand nigger—one of them who never
freckled during recess, smelled of curry

and spices, ate their sandwiches rolled up
in brown bread, skin dark as almonds.
Except they got it wrong. No matter how

many times they rode by, chasing us
with words, with rocks and broken bottles
spitting at our backs, they got it wrong.

It was a sign of being blessed after temple,
of celebration when women wore them, red-gold
to match silver-threaded saris, to match red and green

glass bangles that shivered up their forearms, my brother's
jagged, glittering more than a pundit's thumbprint,
more than a holy mark, glittering.

Echo

I cannot make it lovely,
this story of my father: his body
raw under the lights like a skinned

almond, surrounded by sandalwood,
pickled carrots, and the hush
of rice settling in a bag.

I can't help it, I need metaphors:
his body curls like the curve of a cheek,
a knife lies beside him, done with its work.

This story in metaphors. Not simply:
You lie on the floor. You've been cut
by two men you don't know. They wanted

money and you were too slow, didn't understand.
But rather: bruises braid his skin, the bitter black
of leaves, eyes red as the swollen sting

of chili powder. *Why do I write into the past?*
He smells only sweat, sickened blood seeping,
nothing familiar—not black and red pepper pinched

into the air, not the jasmine of his mother's
kitchen. Nothing—until his breath is like a tea
bag twisted, pressed into the cup of the room.

But it's not an Indian grocery, it is a shabby
downtown hotel, the kind that lock their doors
at ten, have security guards to stop the prostitutes

from coming in, from warming themselves
in the lobby. The kind where hallways echo
of accents. The phone is off the hook.

Not, *why do I write about the past?* but, *what story
must I tell?* You lie there dreaming, but I'm
not sure, dreaming of your childhood in Lahore:

the city escaping the finite lines of a map, erased
by riots, civil war. You remember the hot nights,
chattering birds—how the world was never silent then.

You tell me over and over but I can't write it:
the same story, but I know we are leaving
things out. Embellishing. What they must

have said, the words, harsh like Bengali, you never
tell, the first cut and then the next, how you fell
like a sack of mangoes into a heavy tumble.

You have left the spaces empty for me to add
in colors, the smells, to translate to English.
To translate into the present, into beautiful.

Evening Prayer

1.

Two Gods: the one in the closet
and the one from school days
and both are not mine. I opened
the door on God at dusk and closed

him the rest of the day. He perched
on the ledge above my father's shirts
and wool suits, a *mandir* in every Hindu
house, ours smelling of starch, surrounded

by ties and old suitcases. I was the ghost
at school, sat on the pew and watched
as other girls held God under their tongues.
My lips remember the prayer my parents

taught me those evenings with their bedroom
closet open—Ganesh carved in metal, Krishna
blue in a frame. I don't remember the translation,
never sure I really knew it. I got mixed up sometimes,

said a section of the "Our Father" in the middle
of the *arti,* ending in Amen when I meant *Krishna,
Krishna,* not sure when to kneel and when to touch
someone's feet with my hands.

2.

My name means it all—holiness, God, evenings
praying to a closet. My mother says before I
was born, I was an ache in the back of her throat,
wind rushing past her ear, that my father prayed

every evening, closet door open, for a daughter.
And so I am evening prayer, sunset and mantra.
At school, I longed for a name that was smooth
on the backs of my teeth, no trick getting it out.

Easy on the mouth, a Lisa or a Julie—brown hair
and freckles, not skin the color of settling dusk,
a name you could press your lips to, press lips
against, American names of backyard swings, meat loaf

in the oven, not of one-room apartments
overlooking parking lots, the smell of curry
in a pot, food that lined the hallways with its
memory for days. I watched the hair on my legs

grow dark and hated it. I longed to disappear,
to turn the red that sheened on the other girls
in school, rejecting the sun, burning with spite.
In the mirror, I called myself another, practicing—

the names, the prayers, fitting words into my mouth
as if they belonged: *Ram, Ram* and alleluia, *bhagvan,*
God the Father, thy will be done *Om shanti, shanti, shanti.*